# THE HUNT CONTINUES

The iconic *Predator* series of movies has been a box office success story for over 30 years. Now, *The Predator* presents a bold new vision of one of cinema's greatest monsters.

*The Predator: The Official Movie Special* offers an in-depth look at the creation of the movie as the cast and crew tell the story of how they brought the Predator back to Earth...

**TITAN EDITORIAL**
Editor Jonathan Wilkins
Senior Editor Martin Eden
Assistant Editors Tolly Maggs & Jake Devine
Art Director Oz Browne
Contributor Darren Scott
Senior Production Controller Jackie Flook
Production Supervisor Maria Pearson
Production Controller Peter James
Senior Sales Manager Steve Tothill
Subscriptions Executive Tony Ho
Direct Sales & Marketing Manager Ricky Claydon
Advertising Assistant Bella Hoy
Commercial Manager Michelle Fairlamb
U.S. Advertising Manager Jeni Smith
Publishing Manager Darryl Tothill
Publishing Director Chris Teather
Operations Director Leigh Baulch
Executive Director Vivian Cheung
Publisher Nick Landau

**DISTRIBUTION**
U.S. Newsstand: Total Publisher Services, Inc.
John Dziewiatkowski, 630-851-7683
U.S. Newsstand Distribution: Curtis Circulation Company
U.S. Bookstore Distribution: The News Group
U.S. Direct Sales: Diamond Comic Distributors
For information on advertising contact adinfo@titanemail.com

*The Predator: The Official Movie Special*, published by Titan Magazines, a division of Titan Publishing Group Limited, 144 Southwark Street, London SE1 0UP. For sale in the U.S., Canada, U.K., Eire, Australia and New Zealand.

**ISBN: 9781785866203**

**Printed in the U.S. by Quad**

**First Edition: September 2018**

Thank you to Nicole Spiegel and all at Twentieth Century Fox for all their help.

# CONTENTS

# THE STORY SO FAR...

The mysterious aliens known as Predators have been visiting the Earth to single-out and hunt the strongest and most resourceful humans for a long-time...

## VAL VERDE, 1987

Alan "Dutch" Schaefer, a retired US Army Major, led an elite paramilitary team consisting of mercenaries: Blain, Hawkins, Poncho, Billy, and Mac, on a top secret mission to rescue a government official held hostage by insurgents. An old friend of Schaefer's, former commando and CIA agent Dillon, was enlisted to supervise the team.

As the mission progressed, the team found the twisted wreckage of a helicopter along with skinned corpses. The team killed the insurgents. Dillon admitted that the mission was, in fact, arranged to retrieve intelligence from the captured operatives from the helicopter.

The team captured a guerilla, Anna, and headed to the extraction point. But they were being followed by an unseen figure using thermal imaging. Anna ran away, but just as she was recaptured by Hawkins, the creature struck, killing Hawkins and dragging his body away – but letting Anna live. A search ensued, during which Blain was the next victim. Mac opened fire, wounding the creature.

That night, the creature struck again. Mac mistakenly killed a wild pig in the confusion, and the creature took Blain's body. Poncho was injured during the fight. Mac and Dillon gave chase, but the alien was waiting in ambush and killed them. Billy and Poncho, its next targets, were killed, and Dutch was left wounded. The Major realized that the creature only attacked armed prey, so he instructed the unarmed Anna to get to the chopper.

The creature chased Dutch into a river. However, the water caused its cloaking device to malfunction. Dutch could finally see the creature, and now *he* was cloaked – covered in mud from the riverbank, and he went unnoticed.

The creature realized that Dutch was a worthy opponent. Removing its mask and weapons, it took on the Major in hand-to-hand combat. Dutch finally defeated the creature, crushing it under a trap's counterweight. Dying, the Predator activated a self-destruct unit.

## LOS ANGELES, 1997

Ten years after the events of Val Verde, Los Angeles was in the midst of a heatwave as a turf war raged between Colombian and Jamaican drug cartels.

A Predator watched a gun battle between the police and the Colombians, and saw police Lieutenant Michael Harrigan heroically rescue two wounded officers, temporarily forcing the Colombians off the streets.

The Predator attacked the Colombians. When Harrigan and his police detectives entered the hideout, they found the Colombians dead. Harrigan chased the leader of the gang onto the roof, shooting him when he opened fire on the cloaked Predator.

Jamaican cartel members raided the Colombian drug lord's penthouse, murdering him, but they were subsequently killed by the Predator. Harrigan discovered the Jamaicans' corpses suspended from the rafters. Harrigan met with Jamaican drug lord King Willie. King Willie informed Harrigan of the Predator's supernatural nature. After Harrigan left, the Predator materialized, killing the drug lord.

Following a lead to a slaughterhouse, Harrigan chased the Predator but was stopped by Special Agent Peter Keyes, who revealed the true natue of the Predator. Keyes and his team attempted to trap the creature, but it killed them. The Predator and Harrigan fought onto the roof and eventually into the Predator's ship, hidden below the city. After seeing a trophy room with various skulls, Harrigan finally killed the creature with its own weapon. Other Predators decloaked, and the leader of the aliens presented Harrigan with an old flintlock pistol. As the ship began to launch, the detective escaped. When the remainder of Keyes' team lamented the opportunity to capture the alien, Harrigan remarked, "Don't worry. You'll get another chance..."

And now... The hunt continues...

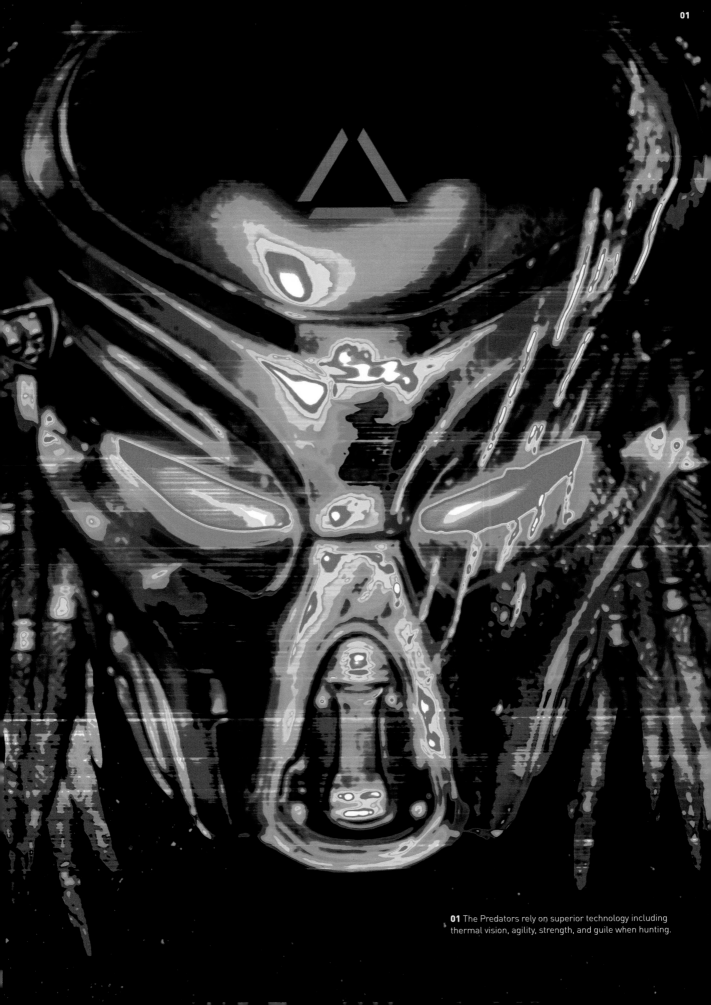

**01** The Predators rely on superior technology including thermal vision, agility, strength, and guile when hunting.

# SHANE BLACK
## THE DIRECTOR

Shane Black first encountered the Predator in the classic 1987 movie, when he played the foul-mouthed radio operator, Rick Hawkins. Over 30 years later, he is now calling the shots as the co-writer and director of *The Predator*.

02

**H**ow did you first get introduced into the world of *Predator*?
I was writing *Lethal Weapon* with [producer] Joel Silver; he had just done the film *Commando* with Arnold Schwarzenegger. *Predator* – or *Hunter* as it was originally called – was to be the next film. It was a lovely script written by two surfers in Newport Beach. Joel and Arnold asked for it to be jazzed up a little.

When did you know that the movie was special?
It was the moment when I saw Arnold Schwarzenegger and Carl Weathers' characters have an argument on screen. I thought, *This isn't like a typical Arnold Schwarzenegger movie. They're actually playing this for real. Arnold's really angry and here, he's really afraid.* The way it was all coming together, and the commitment of those actors and how seriously they were taking it, was really interesting to me. It wasn't a typical Schwarzenegger film with jokes in it.

Why did you want to make this new *Predator* film?
I don't think there has been a *Predator* movie where you really sat up and said, "Oh my god, they're really doing something special." I want people to get their tickets in advance for this one. I want people to know about the movie because they're the fans who, after 30 years of watching *Predator* movies, can say, "Okay, they're taking it seriously now." It's the right time, I think, to resurrect those '80s pictures. It feels like the right zeitgeist for me.

**"IT'S THE RIGHT TIME, I THINK, TO RESURRECT THESE '80S PICTURES. IT FEELS LIKE THE RIGHT ZEITGEIST FOR ME.'"**

Part of me, just for sheer nostalgia, is thinking, *Let's go make the ultimate Summer movie that we like and stuff it with as many kinds of fun genre bits that were our favorite things when we were in high school or college as we can!* It's like going back to a time and a way of thinking and having fun in this genre playground.

What are you doing that pays homage to the original film?
We reference a lot of the stuff from the earlier pictures. Adding Jake Busey [as the son of his father Gary Busey's character, Peter Keyes, from *Predator 2*] to the cast, is a lot of fun. We got the spirit of the hunt in; that's one sort of inviolable rule with the *Predator* movies: you have to frame it somehow as a hunt.

We've looked at the technologies and the behaviors of the Predators to try to go further into what the Predators are like. I think if there was a tagline for this one, it would be, "This time they're hunting their own," which I think is kind of an impressive tagline. It's evocative.

The biggest homage to me is finding the right six guys that bring that same kind of camaraderie. When I was growing up, you hated the idea of the war, it was ▶

**01** Reunited with an old friend, Shane Black at work on set. (See previous spread)

**02** Preparing a scene with Jacob Tremblay (Rory).

**03** Overseeing a complicated piece of action with one of the film's biggest stars!

## "WHEN I WAS GROWING UP, YOU HATED THE IDEA OF WAR BUT THE CAMARADERIE WAS WHAT YOU CELEBRATED. THE EFFORTLESS COOPERATION AND THE TRUST AMONGST THE MEN."

▶ horrible, but the camaraderie was what you celebrated, the effortless cooperation and the trust among the men. And that's what we tried to do – get that group of six guys that reflects in the best way what we found so wonderful about the first *Predator* movie. This group of guys have each others' back, but there's also a sense of quirkiness, commitment, and character.

I think that's probably where I'm most happy; we assembled a group that this time is not comprised of people you would traditionally call action stars, but simply guys who have amazing acting chops. They can act tough and become engaged with each other so that the audience likes them and as they begin to get picked off, you care enough to actually say, "No, not that one!"

It's a war movie. Bad things happen. People will die, and you won't like some of the deaths, but they're all heroes and they can all gauge and relate to each other in ways that make this more than just a monster movie.

**How would you explain the movie to a newcomer to the franchise?**
In this movie, these highly advanced alien creatures, the Predators, have been coming to Earth, and hunting us. It's now not a secret because the government knows what's coming. They've even established a defense agency dedicated solely to preparing us for a Predator incursion. And this movie is about that incident.

Our story is about six guys who aren't government employees. They're forgotten soldiers. They're all broken. I think it's interesting that these sort of oddballs with unbelievable combat skills but attitude problems come together. As opposed to just a crack team of soldiers who are effortlessly good, these guys have to a make an effort to be good, but there's still a spark waiting to be ignited. There's this sort of unquenchable spirit that is flickering but never quite dies out, and this movie is their opportunity to come to life and support each other. They are the least likely people you would ever choose to form a unit and go up against the monster, but they're really tough when the chips are down!

**What made the alien design special?**
It's special because there's a mask that's really cool and then you take off the mask and it's even cooler. It's a creature that we recognize, that walks like us, that understands us, that has the same kinds of primitive impulses as a human being, but it's clearly not from here. And so the ability for a guy to look in the Predator's face and actually relate to it is what's interesting. ▶

**04** Black shows Tremblay around the Predators' ship.

**05** The acclaimed writer/director: "Humor to me has always been a big thing."

**06** Taking a break with actor Boyd Holbrook (McKenna).

The Predator has the capability of being an actual character. I think there's even a way to humanize a Predator and give it a story. There's a scene in the movie where the Predator doesn't have his armor and he's cold, so he's shivering. Predators like heat and they'll put up with pain, but when they're cold they still shiver.

**Have you upgraded the Predator costume for this film?**
I think it's always important to find the coolest variant without violating the basic principle that made the first one popular. I didn't want to go too far because I want it to be nostalgic for that first movie.

I thought, *Let's have one Predator that looks like what we're used to, another that's maybe a little more grizzled, one that's an über Hercules of a Predator...* but so that they don't lose the spark of what was so great about the original Predator, which was that human quality. As deadly as it was, it wasn't just a wild animal, it had an intelligence and a cunning and it could look at you and see what you're afraid of and see how to stop and catch you.

I think our deadliest Predator, the Assassin Predator, is probably the scariest one yet. We worked on the design for a while. Our production designer, Martin Whist, worked really hard on the design – it takes your breath away.

**Would you have been able to make such a realistic creature without the advancements in special effects?**
No, we wanted to meld special effects, visual effects, and practical in the best way. But at the same time we needed to take the Predator to a next level of deadliness that required a degree of computer generated imagery. I don't like to overuse CG. I'm a fan of old school methodologies.

**What drives the Predators to come to our planet?**
We looked at the idea of trophies, collecting the victims' spines, and we thought, *Well, if we're to give these guys an intelligence beyond just this thuggish hunter, someone had to build these spaceships. Somewhere on that planet, there's a society which involves civilized life and science and technology beyond ours.* So given that, we decided to dwell on the fact that Predators are obsessed with survival. One of the things they do on other planets is carry back trophies, which have within them the DNA of every species they hunt from every planet they've hunted. These are the most deadly, adept, and capable examples of that species. They find the best of every planet, rip out its spine, and then isolate traits, in order to upgrade themselves.

**How would you describe the tone of the film?**
Well, we're the R-rated version of *Stranger Things*. We're trying to encompass in one movie all the kinds of genre things that we loved from *Johnny Quest* all the way through *Alien* to Steven Spielberg movies, and never forgetting the realism. So yes, heads come off! These Predators are gonna slice and dice. We have free rein to make a real old school adventure film that sums up for us all the genre tropes that we have grown to love.

> **"THE PREDATORS FIND THE BEST OF EVERY PLANET, RIP OUT ITS SPINE, AND THEN ISOLATE THE TRAITS IN ORDER TO UPGRADE THEMSELVES."**

**07** Black returns to a familar setting some 30 years later, with Boyd Holbrook.

**08** Working on a shot in Rory's basement den with Jacob Tremblay.

**Are you hiding the Predators in the shadows?**
I think part of the fun is seeing a Predator come around the corner and imagining what it would mean to you. There's a noir aspect and a moodiness which I think is important. But in the same way that a lot of movies now linger on the monster, I think one of the more interesting ideas is, in the course of a naturalistic movie, sometimes you'll see the monster but there's someone standing in front of it. Or as they're shooting at it, it crosses and someone walks and blocks it. This gives it more of a documentary feel which is more realistic. In the city, it's a stark, realistic urban environment that includes this creeping presence. If we keep that real enough, maybe you'll buy it when these über Predators start walking out because everything else seems more real.

**Why is injecting humor into the movie important to you?**
I think life is insane and the more cracked and bizarre you make the reality, the more realistic it gets. I like camaraderie. I love non sequiturs. People talking off the cuff, showing grace under pressure, saying deadpan lines in the middle of combat, is what I grew up on.

Shifting tone is important. You make a stew, you want to vary things by putting all the flavors in. So humor to me has always been a big thing. I'm hoping to keep it just funny enough but not that it eclipses the scares. We have to be afraid, we have to be scared of the Predator. We're making a horror movie but if you just stick to the book, you get bored. I want to see life and humor in people. And then once you're engaged, when they start getting sliced and diced, you feel a little bit more aversive to them being in danger than if they had been just stoic, rock-jawed characters throughout.

**What are you most excited about? What has this movie become for you?**

What I'm most excited about in this film is the way that we've had all kinds of genre elements blended together into this stew. This is one more story but encompasses the Predator through the genre, it has all of the different parts you want to see in one movie. I'm excited about the chance to make a playground out of it.

Also, more than being excited, I feel lucky. I mean, I'm truly blessed. To be afforded this opportunity, to be on the map still and viable after 30 years and still operating at this level where budget is this big, stars are this good, and I've been given this much latitude to play in the Predator sandbox, pinch me 'cause I must be dreaming! ⚠

01

# FRED DEKKER
## WRITER

Exploring why the Predator looks like he does is at the heart of *The Predator*. Writer Fred Dekker brings new life to one of the most-feared races in the galaxy...

**H**ow did the initial discussions with Shane Black about doing a *Predator* film start?
Shane wanted to do something that serviced the idea and the mythology in a way that we hadn't seen since the first movie. When he asked me to be involved, I was thrilled because I have a little bit of objectivity about it. I started asking questions about some of my problems with the original movie.

It always bothered me that the Predator was essentially humanoid and that he was bilaterally symmetrical – he had two arms, two legs and a face. I said, "Can we make a plot-point of why that is?" This became a part of the story, so that was very gratifying for me.

**What balance are you trying to make between this film and the original?**
This is a sequel to *Predator* (1987) and *Predator 2* (1991) and it's expanding the mythology. Everything that's in those films still exists, but there's an even bigger puzzle box that we're opening.

**Why was making the Predator more of a character important to you?**
Shane said he wanted to do something that was special, that had a must-see quality about it, and we wanted to expand the mythology. Fans loved the hunter and he's got trophies. We've seen that so much that I began to ask myself, "What do the Predators do besides hunt?"

**What interests you about the Predator?**
We became very interested in what the Predator's agenda is, other than hunting. They've invented interstellar flight so they're not dumb. We also became interested in the idea of different kinds of Predators. We've pushed some envelopes in terms of the existing mythology.

We have Predators with very different agendas. They have different factions within their society that aren't necessarily in collusion – and may even be on the brink of war. That became very interesting because by opening that door, there's a bunch of other doors that we can then go into. ▶

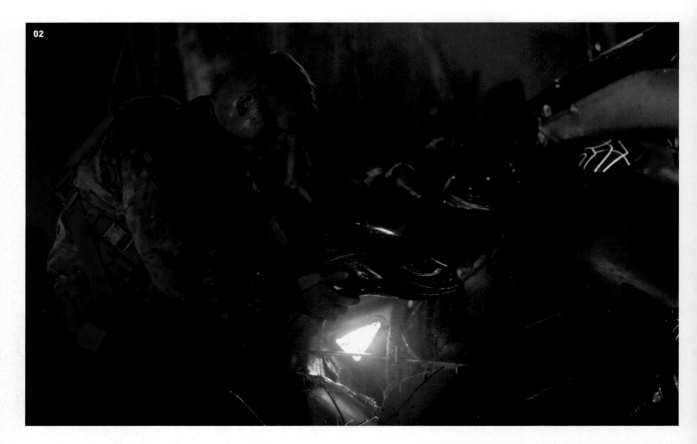

02

▶ **What does the government know about the Predators?**
Our suspicion is that Predators have come here before they met Dutch and his team in the first movie. If that's the case, the government is very probably aware of that and haven't told the public. That was a fun road to go down.

**What is Project Stargazer?**
Project Stargazer was initially imagined by us to be a top-secret government lab – very high tech – in which the Predators that we might capture could be studied. What happened in the back-story of the movie is that the government put it in the hands of the CIA so they could have that cover of plausible deniability. But what they didn't know is that by asking Traeger to take over the operation at Stargazer, he would essentially turn it into a scheme to use Predator technology for profit.

There are two factions in this movie – there are those that we have colluded with, who we are sharing technology and intelligence with. And then there are the others who are using upgrade technology to better themselves, to make themselves more survival machines, to make themselves capable of kicking ass bigger and better than any Predators prior to that.

**How does this upgrade relate to the Predators?**
The Predators only want to hunt the prey that they feel is worth hunting – prey that is a match for them. They've hunted creatures on all planets and presumably handpicked the ones that they find the most challenging.

**01** Fred Dekker, a Predator and Shane Black. (See previous spread)

**02** McKenna (Boyd Holbrook) makes a discovery in the jungle.

**03** The most-feared hunter in the galaxy.

> **"THE PREDATORS ONLY WANT TO HUNT THE PREY THAT THEY FEEL IS WORTH HUNTING – PREY THAT IS A MATCH FOR THEM."**

What they're doing is extracting the DNA to upgrade themselves, so they've got the DNA of all the great hunters, survivors, and creatures throughout the universe.

**Have they taken up some characteristics of those?**
Yes, which goes back to my obsession with explaining why the Predator in the first movie is humanoid. It's possible that they started these experiments early on and the Predator in the first movie may have had some element of human DNA itself, and that the original Predators looked very different.

**Why do you think the Predator in the first film is one of cinema's most iconic creatures?**
The design is so elegant and all the great monster designs immediately target our subconscious. We look at this creature and we see some mirror image of ourselves but in a dark, scary, primal way – it's hard to create something like that. I'm told that James Cameron came up with the mandibles on a plane flight with Stan ▶

## "OUR LEAD CHARACTER, MCKENNA, IS MESSED UP A LITTLE — AND THEN HE'S CONFRONTED WITH PREDATORY ALIENS FROM ANOTHER WORLD…"

► Winston. That's very iconographic. The dreads are very iconographic. It's not a generic alien.

**What's McKenna's backstory?**
Our lead character, Quinn McKenna, is an army sniper and you have to have a very strange worldview, I think, to take that job. He's got a broken marriage, he's estranged from his son, he's messed up a little – and then he's confronted with predatory aliens from another world. He's got a lot of heart and he's got a lot of soul but he's also a soldier and there's something really powerful about that combination.

McKenna is not really comfortable in his own skin. He's happier behind a sniper scope than he is having to deal with his son and his wife, and that makes it all the more touching that he becomes the leader of this dirty dozen. Boyd Holbrook is astonishing as McKenna.

**Why did you decide to give Quinn's son a medical condition and how did that develop their stories?**
Shane Black has always been interested in characters who are a little bit out of the mainstream, and I'm always interested in the outcasts. So what's touching about McKenna is that he's equipped to kill an enemy at 500 yards with a rifle, but his son being on the autism spectrum scares him.

He's not comfortable walking into that house and seeing his wife and having to deal with his son. But one of the things that I believe about movies is they should always be the most important thing that happens in somebody's life. We should really be seeing them at the pinnacle or at the depths of a situation. What this story pushes him to do is to realize that life's short and that his relationship with his son is important.

**Why is it important to have a female character that's elusive and smart with attitude?**
It is no surprise for me to say that female characters have gotten a raw deal in movies from the beginning. Casey was a character that I brought to the table. I was really enamored and interested in showing a woman who's every bit as good as the guys, who can give as good as she gets and is smart and funny.

I don't think she's had a lot of successful relationships because she falls in love with people who aren't as smart as her, and who she immediately knows what they're doing and realizes that it's not worth it. All of our characters have an undercurrent of unhappiness and that makes the whole movie better because it's anchored in a human reality. ►

**04** A Predator takes control aboard its ship.

**05** Quinn McKenna is reunited with his ex-wife.

**06** Casey is pushed to the limit.

> "I THINK ANY MOVIE NEEDS TO HAVE A HUMANITY. YOU NEED TO CARE ABOUT THE CHARACTERS OR IT DOESN'T MATTER WHAT THE STORY IS."

It was a conscious decision that Casey's not going to just be a love interest. She's a scientist, she's funny, she's weird, she likes animals more than people, and she's our co-lead in the movie. I was very happy with the character on the page and I'm thrilled with what Olivia Munn's done with it.

**Why is this group of people so willing to throw themselves behind McKenna to attack the Predator?**
When we were writing the film, we actually struggled a lot with, "Why would the Loonies join up with McKenna and become a part of this mission, which is extremely dangerous and in fact costs some lives?" In this instance, this ragtag group had been in counseling at the Veterns Administration prior to McKenna meeting them, and the problem was that they didn't have a mission. Being outcasts from society, they want a reason to *be* and they want something to do. The truth is that McKenna gives them a reason. He gives them a mission and that's what they were looking for.

**What have you seen from this group that made them collectively feel like a fun team?**
Shane goes out of his way to service all of the actors and he's very sensitive to when he feels like one or some of them are just standing there – particularly with the caliber of actors we have. Trevante Rhodes plays Nebraska Williams. He's coming off a spectacular performance in *Moonlight* and is a serious, fine actor. Keegan-Michael Key, same thing. He's a whirlwind, and he brings such great humor, lightness, and energy.

And when you have all these people who bring different things, it's like the lightning in a bottle analogy. We've been really lucky, because they're all really good people and nobody wants to be in the spotlight on their own. You've got Thomas Jane and Keegan-Michael Key playing up over there and Augusto is over here, and Alfie Allen is eating pickles... It's crazy! Trevante is sitting there with that smoldering presence, and Boyd too with this leadership quality... With them just sitting watching these buffoons, it balances the scene and gives it kind of a gravity that otherwise would spin it out of control.

If you listen carefully, you'll hear Trevante coughing throughout the movie. Nebraska has lung cancer and I just thought that was brilliant because, to me, with pulp action-adventure comic book movies, the more there's a reality to them, the more that you can see real life and real people in them, the better they are. And that was a wonderful actor taking a line and turning it into a character.

**07** The Predator at work in the lab.

**08** McKenna borrows some high-tech weaponry.

**What does a *Predator* movie need to stay true to being a *Predator* film?**
To stay true to its roots, a *Predator* movie needs to be scary. It needs to have a sense of menace, of a hunt occurring throughout the film. There is going to be a certain amount of bloodshed, and there will probably be some viscera and goo as well.

I think any movie needs to have a sense of humanity. You need to care about the characters or it doesn't matter what the story is. So that was the first flag we planted.

**How does the set bring the script to life?**
When I walked onto the Mexican cantina set, it was exactly what I had seen in my mind's eye when I wrote that first scene. So you've got that set and that vibe. You've got Project Stargazer which is a James Bond set but even more high tech. So you've got this lab under a dam, and you've got the Mexican cantina, and then we go inside the Predator ships which [Production Designer] Martin Whist has created spectacularly.

What's exciting to me is that all of those sets and all of that iconography and feeling are in the same movie. This is not a one-note movie - we've got a 10-year-old character on the spectrum who's one of our leads, we've got this smart, brassy, beautiful woman who's one of our leads, and then we've got these crazy servicemen. I just love the variety of it. I love the colors of it. It's a ride in every sense.

**How did you approach the absurdity of the storyline and make it believable?**

I believe there's movie logic and there's real logic. This is why I love *Breaking Bad* so much. Every time something bad happens in that show, it has a ripple effect and we see what would actually occur if that door was opened and those dominoes fell. That's really hard to do. Real logic is when James Bond drives a boat through the bayou and crashes through a wedding. The insurance agent is going to be called, and the families will be very upset. But you don't show that part.

So the reality of this, it's a *Predator* movie. The important thing is that it has an emotional root - that at the base of it are characters that you like, that amuse you, and you have an emotional involvement with or empathize with. If you care, everything else will work.

**What are you most proud of so far?**

I'm most proud of how little *The Predator* has changed from our initial idea. Even though it's changed for budget reasons, casting, things we couldn't quite pull off – Shane's eyes tend to be bigger than his stomach on everything we've ever done. But it's very true to our first instinct of what we set out to do.

And something else that I really strongly believe is that creativity is largely subconscious. We just follow our gut. And so it's constantly changing, it's fluid but very organic. Shane's passionate about his work. And if he's not interested he doesn't touch it, and if he is interested he's all in. That's very empowering. ⚠

# PREDATORS
## A CREATURE FEATURE

With crab-like faces and trailing dreadlocks, the Predators are amongst the most recognizable movie aliens. But for *The Predator*, the designers were tasked with creating myriad terrifying creatures.

**H**ow did you create the new Predators?

**Alec Gillis (Co-designer/creature builder):** We were tasked with designing three very different-looking Predator characters. We based one on the original Predator – not to exactly duplicate every detail and every spine and dreadlock, but to say, "This guy represents that original type of Predator." Then we had two others that we were calling "the emissaries." We started off with the idea of making them older, but in the end we went in a different direction and youthened those Predators up.

We also gave them different color schemes to help separate them. One is much paler, and he's got more purples on him. The other one has more greens and browns. Overall, we were very pleased that production gave us the resources to create three different characters as opposed to saying, "Well, you've got the sculpture of one – just make more and paint them differently."

Did Shane Black have any specific ideas for you?

**Tom Woodruff (Co-designer/creature builder):** In our earliest meeting with Shane, he brought us some ideas that he wanted to see explored. For the two 'new' Predator characters, he initially said, "Let's think of them as scientists." And that, to us, meant, "OK, how do we make them appear as non-tribal as possible?" At one point, they were going to have the equivalent of a lab coat in the Predator world. They would look like they are helping this contingent of American soldiers or think tank. It helps to have those early talks as we're creating the look, the sculptures, suits and animatronics of the creatures.

Why is the Predator such a believable design?

**AG:** What's still wonderful about the original design of the Predator is that it is basically a humanoid. It's relatable in that respect. It has a culture, and it has a code, and hunting skills. But it's got a bizarre face. It's just a creepy combination of amphibian and crustacean and human. It's so weird and bizarre.

Which elements of design did you have to stay true to?

**TW:** With any character, particularly a creature character that was so well designed and well-loved to start with, there are signature aspects that we knew we had to keep. We knew the Predator's emissaries would have dreadlocks, to some level. ▶

02

## "[THE PREDATORS] HAVE A CULTURE, A CODE, AND THEY HAVE HUNTING SKILLS." - ALEC GILLIS

► We experimented with different ideas, like using very clear, translucent dreadlocks. We also tried using some flat dreadlocks. We tried a bunch of different things before we arrived at the final look, but we knew it was important that they have dreadlocks. It was equally as important that they have the crab mandibles. We changed the teeth a little. Our Predators have much more translucent skin. Those hallmark elements are there, but there's a slight organic variation to them. We made their bodies much leaner. They're not the big, muscle-bound warriors, whether by choice of what they've done with their lives or by design. They have genetically enhanced themselves in all kinds of ways. They have much sleeker, more streamlined bodies.

**Why does the Predator costume work so well as a design?**

**Alec Gillis:** Part of its success is that it's based on the human form. We start with body casts of 7ft tall guys, then we work from the proportions they bring to it. We try not to make the suits too bulky because movement is the key. It's the same thing with the face. Eye-spacings are different on different people. So, you automatically get a different look for each Predator, which is just what nature gives you.

Olivia Munn said, "When you stand in front of a Predator, it's so impactful, it's so creepy, it's so scary." And that's how an actor thinks, because acting is reacting. If you're reacting to an actual thing that's looking at you, roaring and drooling, you're going to give a very different performance than if you're asked to look at a green tennis ball on a stick. That's very valuable, not just for the actors but for the audience as well. If it's performed by real human beings, it feels more real.

**01** A classic Predator. (See previous spread)

**02** Alec Gillis at work on a Predator mask.

**03** A close-up look at Gillis and Woodruff's Predator headpiece.

**04** The giant upgrade Predator is prepared for a take.

# UPGRADE PREDATOR

**Martin Whist (Production designer):** Stan Winston is a genius and his original Predator design is timeless and iconic. We wanted to advance the Predator's technology, and maybe its suit. I don't think that it was a huge departure. The fundamental makeup of the face, and the mandibles, and the dreads are all there. This Predator just happens to be advanced biologically as well. His body becomes armor when he is in combat mode. He's a tan, Earth tone color when he's calm, but gets black and red war stripes when he's not. He becomes really menacing. He's the baddest of the badass.

We've done everything we can to be true to the original designs, but we wanted to offer a new advancement with this upgrade. I hope that people like it because we sure do, and I think it will be a little surprising...

# BRIAN ALEXANDER PRINCE
# "PREDATOR"

A former competitive basketball player, Brian Alexander Prince is now the world's tallest parkour practitioner, and he's recently had stunt roles in *Black Panther*, *Captain America: Civil War* and *The Walking Dead*. With a body that size that can move the way it does, it seems only natural he'd be the man to step into that iconic costume and play the galaxy's deadliest Predator...

**W**hat are the challenges of being a Predator?
The *Predator* team told me what to be prepared for in terms of the heat, because it gets super-hot in the suit. I actually wasn't too concerned about that as I'm from Georgia, and it gets really humid there in the summer. But the suit was hotter than I ever could have imagined!

It definitely surprised me with how much the Predator suit loosened up, because in the beginning it was really tight. It's all made out of foam, and the armor is made out of 3D printed plastic. At first, everything was really restrictive; it was really hard to move in it. But as the weeks went on, I got stronger and adjusted to the suit a lot more.

There were still some other things that caught me by surprise that I wasn't at all prepared for. I wore these Predator feet with claws on them and I could feel those nails digging into things when I was walking. I had a whole team of people that helped me put on the suit, kept the costume in check, made sure my dreads looked wet, and so on. They were amazing – I couldn't do anything without them!

This kind of role is so new for me, and there were a lot of moments where I'd be fully suited up and ready to go, and then hours would go by. Then "Action" comes and you have to act like you haven't been struggling for the last two hours. So these elements of getting into character and acting were totally new for me, and that was probably one of the hardest things for me to get used to.

What kind of physical background do you have?
I've been doing parkour for nine years, and last year I actually worked in Seattle at a parkour gym. I had done a few stunt jobs in Atlanta when I lived there. Then one day I get a call and it was Lance Gilbert, the *Predator* stunt coordinator, saying, "Someone told me you were 6'10 and do parkour.."

So I sent him a video of me doing parkour and then they flew me out to LA for an audition at this parkour gym called Tempest Freerunning Academy. I'd always wanted to go there so it was a cool win/win!

▶

## "THERE'S A SCENE WHERE I'M IN THE BACK OF A TRUCK AND I'M FIGHTING SIX GUYS WITH 65 POUNDS ON MY ENTIRE BODY..."

06

▶ I get to LA and they said, "You guys are auditioning for the role of Predator", and it still really hadn't hit me until that moment.

Lance was saying that they were looking for something a little more mobile in the creature and it was a really cool audition. I basically thought, *Okay, I'm just gonna do what I do and see if they like it*. I tried to do what I do, but with a lot of animal to it, and I had this hunting dog thing going on – it was fun. Then the next day I was hanging out in LA and they called me back and they're like, "Yeah we want to give you the Predator role!"

What has surprised you the most about the role?
Mainly how physical it's been. There's a scene where I'm in the back of a truck and I'm fighting six guys with 65 pounds on my entire body – ten of it on my head! I'm squatted down to a half squat so I can fit in the truck, and then the mask is weighing me forward and the lenses are completely fogged up – almost 100 percent.

The reality of it is that there are complications, but we need to make it work. My reach is extended with my fake nails, and I'm behind this layer of mask, so I'm trying to get as close as I can to hitting these guys without hitting them, but it needs to be believable. So there are a lot of these mental gymnastics. I'm in this suit with all these blocks and restrictions and options and things I have to consider. In the beginning, it was super overwhelming. ▶

07

**06** The movie's huge Predator – played by a huge actor!

**07** The Predator takes down another victim.

**08** Even the actors inside the Predator suits can barely recognize themselves.

## "WE WALKED OUT OF THE TENT WEARING OUR PREDATOR SUITS FOR THE FIRST TIME AND EVERYONE FREAKED OUT!"

▶ How well can you hear when you're in the costume?
There's an earpiece with the non-mechanical head – it's kinda fuzzy, like having your hands over your ears. But with the mechanical head, there's nothing. Once they turn on the motors that make the facial features move, that's all you hear and it's just another one of those restrictions! The noise drowns everything out and you just play off of what you're seeing. Then there's also these contact lenses that I wear that make all the colors bright, and it makes everything kinda foggy.

Did you know how terrifying the costumes would look?
No, I would see it in pieces when I did fittings. I saw it when it was just the unpainted body, and then I saw it when it was barely painted, and I saw the head when stuff needed to be clipped off.

And then we did our first camera test. They put the suit on me and it felt a weird amount of ridiculous! I could hear myself breathing – I couldn't open my mouth and it felt weird. The thing that really sells the suit is when they put this layer of slime over the skin and they spray the dreadlocks with water. There's a sheen and a sweaty look to it that's kinda cool.

I remember we walked out of the tent wearing our suits for the first time and everyone freaked out. They were legitimately not faking it! I guess I looked pretty scary… I went in and did my scene and Shane gave me really cool feedback. But I still didn't see how good it was until one of the costuming girls on my team took a picture and showed me. I just look like a completely different person – it's surreal. ▶

**09** Man versus Predator.

**10** Taking command of the ship.

11 The Predator at the controls of its ship.

12 The crew makes sure the Predator is at his best!

## "BEING AS TALL AS I AM AND GETTING TO HAM IT UP HAS MADE FOR SOME OF THE MOST FUN SCENES I'VE EVER BEEN IN."

▶ **What's been the most fun aspect of working on *The Predator*?**

I've done a little bit of stunt work before this but I've never done real acting work. I just loved doing the scenes where I'm in the chair and I get up and I'm pressing buttons and looking over... And then I'm in the suit looking threatening, or where I'm standing on top of the RV and holding Augusto [Aguilera, Nettles] and looking intimidating... those scenes were amazing!

Being as tall as I am – especially in the Predator suit – and getting to oversell it and ham it up has made for some of the most fun scenes I've ever been in. And working with the other actors, doing big scenes and interacting with them has been great. We did this scene where we walk into the ship, we're walking around and I was looking at Trey's character, Williams – he's right in front of me in this scene and I was just staring him down and he's staring me down and it's crazy. It's so much fun!

**What was it like for you to play a creature that big?**

It was crazy. It's just a massive dude! It's more than just the height – it looks powerful, it looks threatening, it's scary and it's intimidating. It's something you don't want to be on the opposite side of a fight with. The suit definitely helps you mentally realize how to play the role. I'm not afraid of it, but at the same time, I definitely felt, "this is gonna be hard!"

▶

▶ Why do you think the Predator creature itself is so scary and iconic?

Because it looks so similar to a human. The Predator is bipedal on its feet, with five-fingered hands, two eyes... You recognize its silhouette as human – but it's more than human. He's huge – he has huge muscles, he has these mandibles for the face... It's clearly alien, but it's not so far removed from being human.

I think something that's even more scary about the Predator is this element of being a feral human creature, but they're actually really smart. It's this really strange mix of being primal; it's wearing a loincloth and it has claws and it's an animal, but at the same time, it has a spaceship and lasers and so it's this crazy mix of old and new. It's scary; it's unpredictable. It's smart, but at the same time, it looks like it's gonna rip your spine out! ⚠

**13** The Predator – don't make him angry...

**14** A Predator cools off between takes.

**15** The iconic, smart yet feral Predator.

# BOYD HOLBROOK
# QUINN MCKENNA

*Playing a mercenary who inadvertently puts his son in harm's way,*
*Boyd Holbrook goes toe-to-claw with brutal creatures from another world.*

**Prior to signing up for this film, what did you know about the *Predator* franchise?**
*Predator* is a legendary film. It's like *First Blood* and *The Terminator*, and all those classic 80s films. It stuck around this whole time as well. So, it's an honor and a privilege to get to work with Shane Black after 30 years, and to reinvent it.

**What makes the Predator so iconic?**
It's a human figure, spatially. It's reptile, but it mimics us. It's more powerful, more methodic, it's more like a stealth warrior. I think it's overpowering. It's like an animal. It's more predatory in the sense of being like a cat, hunting. It's unpredictable, and unlike anything else.

**How was it when you saw the creature on set for the first time?**
It's phenomenal that there are guys working inside the costumes creating the face and the robotics to make the Predators move. These guys are massive! They're seven foot tall, and they're in a full suit.

**What excited you about coming into this franchise?**
That it was very different. We have a main character, we have a group of men, and other elements of the original but it's been reinvented. It's about rooting for people in relationships. For example, McKenna's son and wife are estranged from him; this is no longer just set in one location; the story deals with characters like Coyle and Baxley, and learning how they wound up in the Veterans Hospital, and discovering more about them. At the core of it is something that's real. So, all those things attracted me to it.

To make an action film is one thing. To make an action thriller is something else entirely. Shane Black can hinge all the scenes with our characters on something, and then he adds these little bits of comedy to break the tension. Having all these dynamics in play is something that I have never done. It was a whole different ballgame.

**What is Shane Black's approach to relationships and character development?**
It's important, especially because the dynamic of the story is about a father and a son. McKenna is a father who's detached from the world; he's doing mercenary work in Mexico. Having that much detail written into a character – and how that story is written – is essential.

It's a constant – in every story there's an anchor, something that roots it to the pivoting point of a story. The dynamic – which Shane is so great at – is this circle of the different people ricocheting off of each other – they're jumping on board with McKenna to help save his son. In turn, McKenna's journey goes from not being a father, not being responsible, being estranged from his wife, to becoming a leader, and becoming a father again, and having a sense of purpose.

**Where do we find Quinn when the movie opens?**
When you first meet Quinn he doesn't really have much to live for. He's estranged from his wife and his son, and out on a mercenary job in Mexico when a Predator spaceship crash-lands. McKenna's not aware of the original Predator or the characters in that film. The government knows that happened, and that's been covered up. There have been Predator sightings back and forth, and he stumbles across this. He needs proof or no ▶

▶ one will believe him, so he ends up trying to get this device that he's found back to the states.

**How does Rory become involved in the story?**
Rory is on the spectrum with Autism. In certain forms of Autism there are more advanced interests with numbers, or counting, or remembering. This makes things even worse when he finds the Predator's gauntlet and begins to actually figure out how it works. He begins to put the puzzle together, which, through his own innocence and curiosity, starts an avalanche of problems.

**What was the dynamic like between the actors?**
We had a strong dynamic on set. There were several extremely talented actors all coming from different backgrounds. Keegan-Michael Key is from a classical stage background and Augusto Aguilera is a young, brilliant actor who was in *Moonlight*. It's the chemistry between us all that really started igniting fires and driving things. We all have some amount of experience,

> **"THESE GUYS ARE ROUGHNECKS. THEY KNOW THE CODE. THERE'S A PHILOSOPHY TO BEING A SOLDIER."**

but we all just tried stuff out until we had a really strong form, and once it felt great, we shot that.

**What's the backstory of the "Loonies?"**
They've been doing a little bit of group therapy together. They're all dealing with what they have, whether it be Post Traumatic Stress Disorder (PTSD), or other conditions. But, they're very familiar with themselves, so McKenna has a hazing introduction with these guys. You have to break somebody in if you want to come into the group. From that point, McKenna gets intercepted by Traeger and Stargazer to hush him up.

What is it about McKenna's personality that lets him pass that test?

It takes a soldier to know a soldier. According to the training that I looked into, when you're put against conditions like this constantly, there's a certain amount of detachment and a wicked sense of humor about it. These guys are roughnecks. They know the code. There's a philosophy to being a soldier, and I think in turn that also makes them get on board when they know the reality of what's about to happen to Rory if they don't do something. There's a distinctive emotional charge that they all share.

How does McKenna feel about the Predator hunting Rory?

I think one of the most distinctive things of the story is that it's about the unity of family. Shane usually makes stories about characters with depth, who are struggling with something their own internal way. A lot of McKenna's unhappiness comes from being estranged from his son. There's a primitive sensibility of it all, that if you mess with my kid I'll fight back. I think a lot of people can relate to that.

How does McKenna relate to Rory?

McKenna's conflict with his son is that he is a hard-nosed guy. He doesn't really know how to deal with his son, because he's not emotionally relating. Autism is a very hard thing to talk about, but it is a reality. McKenna has a hard time coming to grips with it. I think that actually has an effect on his son. He doesn't realize that because he's basically too much into his own thing, and he's not giving his son enough attention.

What are your thoughts on the Assassin Predator?

He's a big son of a bitch! This Predator was 11 foot! You should have seen them on set. It looked really crazy. From the torso to the head, it was as big as me. It's an amazing piece of design. The sculptures and the robotics were incredible. ▶

**01** Boyd Holbrook as Quinn McKenna. (See previous spread)

**02** McKenna on his way home.

**03** Holbrook relaxes on the jungle set.

**04** The Predator and his prey? McKenna has an unpleasant alien encounter.

## "THE ASSASSIN PREDATOR WAS 11 FOOT TALL... FROM THE TORSO TO THE HEAD, IT WAS AS BIG AS ME. IT'S AN AMAZING PIECE OF DESIGN. THE SCULPTURES AND THE ROBOTICS WERE INCREDIBLE."

▶ **How did Olivia Munn fit in?**
Olivia's one of the guys. She can hold her own for sure. She's sparky. She's got a very sharp personality. And she plays such a crucial character to this – if it wasn't for Casey we'd be lost.

**What do you think the fans will think of the movie?**
They will be blown away! Everything's new, everything's fresh. Hats off to the previous movies, but we're playing our own story. This is some of the coolest work that I've ever been a part of.

**How does the original *Predator*'s style compare to the kind of characters that Shane usually creates?**
It is quite camp and cheeky. But I think there's been a totally new approach here, still with very definitive characters. The only definitive thing in the '80s was cosmetic work and stuff like that.

**What aspects of this script resonated with you?**
I think it had everything. You want to make people laugh. You want their hearts to sink when Rory is snatched up by a frightening goddamn ugly space alien. It wasn't too serious in certain moments, but it's straight down the barrel at other times. I love that unpredictability of Shane's work. He has that purity and originality as a filmmaker.

**What kind of preparation did you do?**
I was really fortunate to meet a stunt guy on *Logan* who was an ex-sniper out of the SEALs. I was able to hang out with the guy, and he got me on the beach at 5 a.m. in the water, running, and training. I did that for a couple months, and I just got to know these guys. What do they go through in order to do what they do? I thought it was really important to me to understand that sensibility of how these guys have this morbid sense of humor. They have a disconnect – worrying about deaths is a lot more work than just doing it. These guys are a really fascinating group of men.

**Did the physical training help you at all during the shoot?**
Yes. There was a situation where I was going through these bleachers and my foot got snagged. I don't know how it happened, but I didn't zip my shoes up on the

05

06

side. I was falling and my ankle was about to break. But I was just able to pivot out of it. Things like that will shut down a production in a heartbeat.

**Have you done much stunt work previously?**
Nothing too crazy. It gets to a certain level when you're doing wire work. I think I got kicked in the ribs a couple of times, just by accident.

**What's the coolest thing about doing a movie like this?**
It's that you have no clue what you're getting yourself into! I'm a trained stage actor, but when I entered Shane's world, all that went out the window. It was either sink or swim.

On my first day, Thomas Jane, Keegan-Michael Key, Trevante Rhodes, and I rehearsed, and talked a lot. Shane went to his trailer for lunch. He came back with two new pages and said, "We're shooting this in 20 minutes!" ⚠

**05** McKenna is brought in for questioning.

**06** McKenna doing what he does best as he defends his son from the Predator.

**07** The Predator closes in on McKenna, Casey and Rory.

# OLIVIA MUNN
# DR. CASEY BRACKET

Actress and model Olivia Munn is no stranger to playing a hero, having appeared as Psylocke in the recent *X-Men* movies. In *The Predator*, she's a very different hero as Dr Casey Bracket, who's waited her whole life for the call to tell her that humans have come into contact with alien life. It's a call Casey might regret taking...

**What did you know about the *Predator* franchise before signing on to this film?**
I watched the original film, but I didn't watch any of the others, which actually worked out well for this movie because it's not a continuation. It's within the world but it's not a direct sequel. So that really helped me out a lot.

**What was your first Predator encounter like?**
The first time that I actually got to see the entire Predator creature fully put together with a moving mouth was on set. We were filming and then they took the cast into this other room to see the Predator. It was wild! I had no idea how alive and real it would be! There is so much computer generated imagery that makes these movies so wonderful and exciting, but it's really great when there's something that's so tactile and right there in front of you. The Predator creatures are so lifelike. The way they breathe and the way the mouth opens up is really convincing. The special effects guys are brilliant.

**Why were you drawn to appear in this film?**
Working with Shane Black was the number one reason why I wanted to work on this film. I think that he's one of the best directors and writers. I have loved his movies for so long. He does something that's really interesting and creative and feels very new. He's always trying to surprise the audience, even if it's just with a line of dialogue. It felt like we're doing an innovative movie because Shane is an actor and a director. We're all finding fun stuff to do to keep it alive and in the moment. I've never seen a huge movie at this scale operate in such an intimate way.

**What was it about your character, Casey, that resonated with you?**
Usually in these movies, Casey would just be a love interest. In a big movie like this – with all these men fighting the alien – she only exists if *he* exists. But in *The Predator*, she's a scientist and she's not just the love interest. I'm really passionate about how women are portrayed in film and TV. That was what interested me the most about this role, knowing that the character is an evolutionary scientist and a biologist. She is someone that is in her own world. She's so passionate about it, which really helps the storyline. She helps figure out what's going on. She's actually needed for her intellect, not because she's just simply a woman.

**What is her role in the film?**
Dr. Casey Bracket is at the top of her field. She's an evolutionary biologist. She is essentially a scientist who researches how creatures change and adapt. She has been in the CIA and is on the government's list of top people to go to if there was ever contact with intelligent alien lifeforms.

**Are the Predators what she expected?**
It's definitely a surreal experience but at the same time, it ignites something inside of her. This is the epitome of what she studies and that is very exciting for her. At one point, she's chasing a Predator to try and capture it, and examine it up close. She feels she might even be able to communicate with it. It's thrilling for her, but at the same time she is in danger and she has to run for her life. There's definitely a mix of joy and utter fear.

▶

# "IT WAS VERY IMPORTANT TO ME THAT THERE WAS A LOT OF DEATH, DESTRUCTION AND BLOOD."

**▶ What did you think when you first read the script?**
When I read the script, what I really loved was the story of the Predators that are on our side. There are these scary-looking, very brutal, very dangerous Predators, but there's something even scarier and more dangerous. I thought that was a really fascinating part of the story. The script asks, *What would that be like if aliens were here on our side going up against the scariest alien of all?*

I loved how we all come from different worlds. You've got my character who's a biologist. And you've got all of the loonies who are from different military groups with different emotional problems going on, and have experienced different kinds of pain and suffering. Then you've got these aliens who are from somewhere completely different as well, yet we all work together to combat this really scary, very intense opponent.

**Actors use a lot of tools to get into character. What has helped you the most?**
Being on the set, it was hard to grasp the scale of these things. The spaceship feels real and the production team actually built an entire forest. They also built a swamp and they used real trees. They created a cliff! Those things really helped to ground me in the reality of the story that we were telling. It also makes the experience much more fun.

**What was it like being on the ship set?**
The ship was really beautiful. It had these really large pieces of steel that were smooth and rounded. There were lights that went all through it, and everything blended together into a really beautiful piece of architecture. It had pods and secret doors.

It felt larger than life, but at the same time was so intimate. It's crazy because the buttons were massive but still too small for the Predator because the Predator is so large. Each button was the size of an iPad! It was definitely an overwhelming, awe-inspiring experience to be inside of the Ark.

**How was Shane Black able to make the Predators seem almost human?**
Shane is not only in the original *Predator* and is not only our director and co-writer of the movie, but he's a huge fan. Shane has spent an exorbitant amount of money on comic books, which I think shows you he is so detail oriented with the Predator.

Shane, of course, thought a lot about how the Predator reacts to cold, whether it wears pants or not, if it has a lizard type skin or if it has netting on it. That's what true fans and lovers of these movies do, they study it. They see all those details. Shane's somebody that really does his research. The movie is a culmination of research and fantasy. There was a lot of love and geeking out over what this all would eventually look like.

**What have you accomplished together in this film?**
It was very important to me that there was a lot of death, destruction and blood in the movie. Thankfully, Shane and I are on the same page with that. My character goes from living in a nice, clean world with her dogs, being an intellect and a scholar, to being broken down and beaten down and exhausted and on top of a Predator ripping its spine out. That's the kind of extreme transition that she goes through!

The fact is that it's so bloody and guttural. I said it should be a hard 'R' rated movie. Please don't pull it back – just shock me! I want to be in the theatre, watching the movie and having to cover my eyes. I think that Shane was on the same page as me. I said that the gorier the fight scenes that the Predators had with each other, and they had with me – the better. The grittier the better. The scarier the better. ⚠

**01** Olivia Munn as Dr. Casey Bracket. (See previous spread)

**02** Casey and friend escape for a moment away from the movie's death and destruction!

**03** A Predator causes havoc for Casey at the lab!

**04** Casey fights back.

**05** Casey in danger as she hangs by a thread.

# JACOB TREMBLAY
# RORY

A recipient of the Critics' Choice Movie Award for Best Young Performer for his role in *Room* (2016), 11 year-old actor Jacob Tremblay has a career that many would envy. His latest role sees him as an unlikely quarry for the Predator.

**What did you know about *The Predator* before working on this film?**
I knew *The Predator* was a big action movie. I'd never seen the movies before. My mom and I did a marathon of the *Predator* movies. They're awesome! My favorite one is the first one.

**Who is Rory?**
Well, Rory really likes chess and goes to a chess club. He gets bullied. He has a basement which has some pretty cool stuff in it. He likes to go in his basement and do puzzles. And he has autism.

**How did you prepare for the role?**
Me and Shane [Black] had a chance to go to the Canucks Autism Center. We made friends and got to hang out with some kids with autism. We went to gymnastics, we played board games, we baked really good cookies, and we learned about all of the facial tics and stims (self-stimulatory behavior).

Meeting children with autism helped me learn about how Rory would act and how he would move, and it helped me learn about all the different stims that Rory might do. Afterwards, me and Shane discussed it and we really created a character.

**How does Rory's Autism figure in the story?**
Rory helps with this Predator situation because he's good at figuring out things like the keypads on the Predator's spaceship and learning their languages.

**What's his relationship like with his parents?**
Rory loves his dad, and his dad's a soldier. So, usually Rory doesn't get to see him. Before his dad went off to

be a soldier, they spent lots of time together. So, they're really connected. Rory's dad always tells him to be a big boy and grow up and to go and do stuff, and be strong. But Rory isn't really the athletic type. He's more into making things and fixing puzzles and chess.

In the movie, Rory hasn't seen his dad in a long time. And then his dad sends him this package. It contains all these cool Predator gadgets. When he gets sucked into this adventure, he gets to see his dad again.

Rory's mom is a really loving mom, and she takes care of Rory. She really tries to encourage him to go out and do stuff like trick-or-treating. Rory usually doesn't want to do that, because his dad is trying to encourage him to be more grown up.

**What makes Rory's basement so special to him?**
Rory's basement is his safe zone. It's where he can be himself. He has all this cool stuff, things that he can make, like these giant robot things, and he has a huge TV. He has chess tables in there. He has four TVs. Everything that a boy like me would want.

**What have you liked about working with Shane Black?**
What I like about Shane is that he's really nice to me, and he's a really good director. He was really good at helping me with my acting, and he's really funny, too. He always made me laugh off set. I remember one time he brought Nerf guns to the production office. So, when we were rehearsing we had Nerf wars! It was really cool.

**What has it been like working with Boyd Holbrook?**
Boyd is really nice to work with, because he's a really helpful actor. He's really funny too. We hung out a lot. ▶

> One time, I invited him to a hockey game, and he invited me to an early screening of *Logan* (*in which Holbrook appeared as Pierce – Ed*).

**Did you get to do any fun action scenes on this movie?**
I got to use a harness a lot. The harness is for when the Predator picks me up and throws me, and also if I'm climbing into something like the Predator spaceship. We practiced using a harness a lot in rehearsals.

I also got to go down this Predator slide thing. It's really fast, and it's also really cool because there are buttons everywhere in the slide.

**What's it like walking through the stage and seeing everything they are building?**
Walking through the studio, we would see all kinds of stuff. There was a huge forest swamp area and the ark [the Predator's ship], and there were RVs and a stargazer. It was just super cool.

**How would you describe the alien stuff?**
It's metal. I think that the Predator mask is just like the mask from the original movies. This gauntlet is too big for my arm, not for anyone else's. It's huge, and it has the Kujhad [the primary device that operates the Predator's ship], which pops out of it. And it has some awesome colors, and the design is so cool.

## "THE PREDATOR MASK WAS REALLY HEAVY. IT WAS HARD TO HOLD MY HEAD UP!"

**What did you like best about the creature?**
It's so scary. It's so tall, and it has big muscles. It has a very scary face, and it has all these cool tools, like a shoulder laser cannon and an invisibility cloak.

**What was it like seeing one of these guys in costume?**
It was like... Holy cow! He was just like I imagined him to be: He was tall, big, and scary looking. So, I walked up to him, and I gave him a fist-bump!

**What do you think about all the mechanical stuff that is used to create the Predator?**
It's awesome, because one time I got to control the face! The guy who operated the face let me control it. So I made the Predator pull a screaming face. And I made him do a mad face. I could move his mouth up and down, and move his eyebrows.

**What excited you about this movie?**
I have a really cool part because I get to do some pretty fun stuff. I get to drive the alien spaceship, and I get to wear the Predator mask. I was really excited to do it. And also there are Predator hybrids in this movie. There's a big upgraded Predator, and then there's also these other cool Predators. It's all in one movie!

**What would you do if you had a 16-foot Predator living in your room?**
I'd use it as my boxing bag! ⚠

**What can the gauntlet do?**
The Predator wrist gauntlet lights up, and there's different versions of this. On one of them it lights up. On the other one, there's no Kujhad. On this other one, the Kujhad's connected. On this other one, you pop the Kujhad out with your hands. And on this other one, you press a button, and the Kujhad pops out. I think that the one where the Kujhad pops out is my favorite.

**What was it like putting on the Predator mask?**
It was really cool! It's not like what you think it's like. When you put it on, it's like you're putting on an actual Predator mask. That's why I think it's so cool. It also lights up. There's a cool scratch on the side of it, and it is awesome. It's really big, too.

It was really heavy. It was really hard to hold my head up, because I would always be, like, leaning to the side and leaning to the other side. And sometimes I'd even fall to the ground.

**01** Jacob Tremblay as Rory (See previous spread).

**02** Trick or treat? Rory heads out for candy.

**03** License to drive? Taking the controls of the Predators' ship.

**04** Rory engages in a game of chess.

**05** Rory examines a Predator's mask.

**06** Rory might be the key to defeat the Predator threat.

# THOMAS JANE
# BAXLEY

As a former soldier, Baxley's got his own demons to fight — not just the ones hunting him down... Thomas Jane, however was only too pleased to take up arms against the Predator.

**What excited you about this film?**
I always wanted to work with Shane Black. I'm a big fan. He asked me if I would play a part in the movie. He said, "I'm doing *The Predator*, and we have this ensemble cast of guys." He explained the story to me and I just said, "Tell me where to be!" I like Shane's sensibility. I like the way he can create a character that feels real and yet it's funny. That's a very hard tone to hit, and when you hit it, it works really well. It's a tone that's particular to Shane.

**How are the characters introduced in the film?**
We meet a bunch of Post Traumatic Stress Disorder (PTSD) guys, who have been going to the Veterans Health Administration hosptial. Some of them are from the Marines, some of them the army, some are Rangers. They're all screwed up from whatever war they've fought in. They're not reintegrated back into society in a way that makes them feel like productive, normal members of society, and that causes a lot of problems.

I thought it was great to take a group that has served their country and done everything right, but been literally just dropped off on a sidewalk. What would happen if these guys were thrust into extraordinary circumstances where they came up against an alien from another planet who is after his own objective?

So they get together for their monthly meeting and their therapy session, and the next thing you know the military have grabbed us, put us in shackles and thrown us on a bus. They throw McKenna on; he's not crazy, he's just seen an alien! That launches us into this grand adventure where the men have an opportunity to put some of their skills as soldiers to work.

In real life, they're antisocial; they can't hold a conversation. Nettles can't talk to women. We've all got serious problems, but when it comes time to engage with an enemy, all that shit goes away. They're like a well-oiled machine.

**What's the background of your character, Baxley?**
Shane told me that he wanted to pair me up with Keegan-Michael Key. He figured that Baxley and Coyle were in the same unit. Shane had the idea that Coyle was involved in a friendly fire incident where the truck got turned around and he opened fire on his own guys. He killed everybody. except for one guy. And that one guy was Baxley.

They hated each other, but had to spend three years together in the courts, giving testimonies. And finally one day, one of them said, "Hey, you wanna get a cup of coffee?" And that started the relationship that they have. I thought that was terrific.

**How do they interact together in the film?**
I said to Keegan-Michael, "Let's roll with this. You've got PTSD. Coyle must be really messed up. You've killed all your own guys, so you're shell-shocked and guilty. Somehow you're feeling like you might get some redemption from my character. How would my character react to all that?" And Shane said, "Oh, you have Tourette's syndrome."

I did a little research and found there is something called "conversion disorder." When something bad happens or you have a traumatic emotional experience, you can take on the symptoms of another disease, and it can happen with Tourette's. So I hit on that. ▶

**01** Thomas Jane as a hardened veteran of war, Baxley. (See previous spread)

**02** Baxley and Coyle's confrontation comes to a head.

**03** Baxley enjoys some fine art.

**04** Jane, Keegan-Michael Key, and Alfie Allen watch as a motion capture sequence is filmed.

**05** "Unless you're engaged with the characters, [everything else] is boring."

▶ After this terrible experience, Baxley, who's always suffered a little with OCD in the first place but been able to control it, develops conversion disorder. So Coyle now feels even more guilty than he did. Baxley just wants to kill Coyle because he drives him nuts. But Baxley also kind of loves him and wants him to forgive himself.

**The film balances large scale action with character-based scenes. Which did you prefer to do?**
The truth is there's action and death and destruction in almost every movie, so that's all fun. But unless you're engaged with the story and the characters, all that stuff's boring. But it's fun to do, and it's fun to watch when it's good. We have got aliens and stuff blowing up and people dying.

It's fun and it keeps the movie active, but I'm most excited about this crackpot group of half-cocked soldiers, who can't really keep it together for 12 hours at a time. When push comes to shove, they're there for their

## "[THE PREDATOR PLANET] IS COOLING DOWN AND OUR PLANET'S HEATING UP, BUT THEY LOVE THE HEAT..."

people and they'll die for them. And that's something very human.

**What was it like seeing the Predators for the first time?**
The Predator costume is a work of genius, or several geniuses. It takes a lot of brilliant people to put together that costume. There's so much that goes in to these costumes and they're probably the price of a large home in Tennessee!

We've got these two incredible actors who are playing a couple of the Predators. They're both well over seven feet tall, and they're both highly skilled with movement.

They trained for weeks getting into the whole Predator mentality and working out how the Predator should move and what would or wouldn't look right. It looked like a blast to do, and the Predator looks like a badass on screen!

As I was watching what they were doing, it really struck me as to what a hard job it was. They were on the set before everybody else, getting their costumes on. They had to go through a physically punishing process to bring this alien warrior from another planet that kills people for fun, to life. I have a lot of respect for what those actors did.

**What is the Assassin Predator like in this movie?**
He's upgraded, so to me it looks like the Predator, but he's 11 feet tall and he's got some fancy tricks. He's frigging huge and looks awesome! It's good because they didn't mess with the look of the creature. It's still the Predator – they didn't try to turn it into some other thing. It's a giant, badass, mother of a Predator!

The idea is that some of the Predators on the Predators' home planet created a giant Predator to kill the other Predators. They did this because the other Predators were trying to warn people on Earth that they were going to be invaded. Their planet is cooling down and our planet is heating up, but they love the heat. So, they want to trade planets, only the humans will just be kicked off into space!

**Did seeing the creatures on set help to put you in the moment?**
Oh yeah! It was great to have them there so that we could work with them on a scene. Of course, a lot of times we'd just be looking at a tennis ball on a stick or a pink "X" on a green screen. Then at other times we just had to look at the First Assistant Director standing there in his red jacket and he's playing the role of the Predator. But when the actors playing the Predators are on set and you actually get to be in the same shot with them, it's fantastic. There's no acting required! ⚠

# KEEGAN-MICHAEL KEY
# COYLE

Despite appearing to be the joker in the squad, Coyle hides a tragic past.
Keegan-Michael Key reflects on coming up against the Predator.

**What was your knowledge of the *Predator* movies before you started working on this film?**
I am actually a very big fan of the *Predator* franchise. I'm one of those people who knows the entire canon.

**What first interested you about this project?**
The thing that interested me the most about the project was the creative team behind it. Knowing that Shane Black was going to be directing the piece was what excited me the most. He's the person that created the buddy cop genre as we know it today and he still has that kind of forward thinking that he had back then. The sense that he would bring something special to *The Predator* was palpable, and that was the thing that really made me want to jump in.

**How does *The Predator* stand up against the other films?**
I think each movie has its own personality. Different films. Different energies. I'm so invested in the mythology of the *Predator* series. There's stuff you get in the *Alien vs. Predator* movies that's really quite interesting. *Predators* (2010) works in its own way, tonally. For *The Predator*, you could only actually go in this direction. Something really different had to happen, given the wide scope of this universe.

**What got you excited about playing Coyle?**
Coyle is a person who's damaged. He has resigned himself to a life that is mundane; a life that is completely diametrically opposed to the life that he lived when he was in the military.

Specifically, there's a story that Shane and I and Thomas Jane, who plays Coyle's best friend Baxley, started shaping together. It was creatively fulfilling to concieve a wonderful backstory. The sense of Coyle being fragile and masking it with a great deal of bravado was a fun challenge to perform. It's an interesting and layered aspect to his character.

**Is Coyle's humor a shield?**
The humor for him is armor. I don't think he's really fooling anybody. He belongs to this group of gentlemen that go to group therapy to overcome Post Traumatic Stress Disorder (PTSD). They are trying to come to terms with the traumas that they went through during war. Coyle has quite an obvious behavior trait that people use to cope: He tries to laugh it off. He thinks the only way to make it through the day is by telling dirty jokes. He wants to fill a room with jocularity so that it lifts up his mood. It's very transparent.

**What's his background?**
There was a tragic event that took place in his life. In the midst of a firefight, he got turned around and he fired on another light armored vehicle that was in his brigade and destroyed it. There were a bunch of men inside the vehicle, and Baxley was one of those men. He survived but the rest of the men perished. So, then there were many years of inquiries.

There was no time to healthily grieve through the tragedy that he caused. That's the big event that took place in his life. It was this horrible mistake. That's what he has to live with. The jokes are a salve or a tonic, but they're not a cure to the pain that lives inside of him. ▶

# "[COYLE HAS] A CLOSE ENCOUNTER OF THE WHACKED-OUT KIND. HIS BRAIN CAN'T FATHOM IT."

▶ **How does Coyle handle meeting an alien for the first time?**
Coyle does not handle his first close encounter of the third kind well. It's a close encounter of the whacked-out kind for him! His brain can't fathom it, and so he cracks a little bit. A guy with dreadlocks who's from another planet jumps up out of our truck! Coyle's very overwhelmed. He does not deal with it with any sense of aplomb at all.

**What happens when the team have their initial encounter with the Assassin Predator?**
That's a different experience. It freaks him out that there is a bigger one. The survival instinct kicks in. All we know is that we're the good guys and the aliens are the bad guys.

There's intrigue between the aliens. There's mass confusion, and I think everyone is just trying to figure out what the next step is. We agree to follow McKenna and help get his kid back. It keeps the adrenaline going. It keeps everybody at their sharpest, because a new element's been added. I don't know anything about these organisms really, other than they kick ass!

**If you had to explain what a Predator looked like to somebody that's never seen one before, how would you describe it?**
It's kind of like a muscular Jamaican bipedal crab. He looks like someone took a layer of skin off of his face, but it didn't hurt, and he just said, "Ah, I'll keep it like this. No big deal." Maybe he woke up a few times in the mirror and scared himself. But the Predators look like a caveman and a horseshoe crab had sex.

**What are the emissaries?**
The emissaries are two of the most intriguing characters in the whole piece. There's this other story that's happening in the *Predator* universe that we don't get to see. It's fascinating; I feel like you could make a whole other movie just about what's going on on the Predators' home planet. There's political intrigue, diplomacy, the question of what the plans are for the leaders on their planet.

I have my own theories. I think there are two factions on their planet. Their world is cooling down, and they're tropical creatures. So, their legislative body is saying that they should come to the Earth, kill everybody, and take over. They've been hunting here for thousands of years. The other faction is saying the humans have been good prey and should be left to live.

These emissaries belong to the latter faction. What happens is the Predators are coming here to try to figure out how to discuss with us that they don't want to completely eradicate all humans, they want to help. It's interesting to consider the Predators as good guys, but also trying to figure out what's in it for them.

**What was it like when you first saw a fully functioning Predator on set?**
My heart did skip a beat because I had already met the man inside the Predator suit. He was a very warm, and very kind gentleman by the name of Brian. He was already seven feet tall, and then he grew five inches taller in the costume! What really got to me is it has these very malleable eyebrows!

It looked so impressive. I wouldn't even consider attacking a creature that looks like that. It's so large and fearsome. The hair stood up on the back of my neck, and I just marveled at the work that went into creating it. It felt like I was looking at an actual organism walking on the Earth.

**Did Shane Black come up with the Predators characters?**
The emissaries have an objective, the original Predator has an objective, the Assassin has an objective. They are really interesting archetypes that are laden with meaning. It made the Predator characters seems very vintage Shane Black to me.

**Was there anything in particular in the script that you thought people would really respond to?**
It's a group film, and that's something that's attractive to me. It's not a mindless movie. You have to use your brain a little bit. I think it's going to have enough of a span that everybody will enjoy it. If you like seeing a severed arm, or people getting their heads chopped off, that's good, but also there's a little bit of intrigue.

It's factions coming together for a cause, as opposed to just a shoot 'em up, or a revenge flick. But it really is its own thing. It could stand alone. If the first movie didn't exist at all, this movie would still work. It's a very exciting roller coaster ride because there's a lot of new elements being thrown at the audience along the way. We believe the audience is smart enough to follow all of it. We're doing our own story. This is some of the coolest work that I've ever been a part of. ⚠

**01** Keegan-Michael Key as Coyle. (See previous spread)

**02** Coyle, Baxley, and Nettles - an unlikely trio.

**03** Baxley and Coyle race into action.

**04** Key smiles between takes as Coyle makes a final stand.

**05** Nebraska Williams and Coyle in a more relaxed mood.

03

04

05

# STERLING K. BROWN
# TRAEGER

A man with a mysterious agenda, Traeger might not be as bad as he first appears. Actor Sterling K. Brown reflects on cursing with Jacob Tremblay and improvising with Olivia Munn.

**What did you know about the *Predator* franchise before signing on?**
I remember the original movie when I was a little boy. The team of Arnold Schwarzenegger, Carl Weathers, Bill Duke, Shane Black... I remember how large Jesse "The Body" Ventura was. I was like, *Wow, will I ever be big enough to be in a Predator film?* The answer is no. I'm not big enough physically, but thankfully they've changed the size that you need to be in order to be in one of the movies!

**What were some of the things that got you excited about being a part of *The Predator*?**
Shane Black, first and foremost. He's a fantastic writer-director. Having seen other films that he's done, I've just admired the hell out of them. I was very glad to have an opportunity to work with him. John Davis is an incredible producer. The creative team behind the project is great. The actual script itself was very different from the original – it's lighter, probably more cynical. It has a greater sense of humor and it's harder to determine who the good guys and the bad guys are.

The cast is fantastic – they are a really wonderful ensemble of actors to be playing with. Traeger is a character very different to anything that folks have had a chance to see me do up to this point in my career. Any time I get a chance to try to surprise people, I want to take advantage of it.

**What were some of the things that you liked about Traeger?**
Traeger seems like he's the bad guy, but I never quite saw him in that way. He just has his own specific needs that aren't necessarily coherent with what everybody else wants. I like the idea of playing someone who's not bad and twirling his mustache, but he's just simply pursuing his own agenda.

**What do you think about the way the Predators are presented in this movie?**
I think it's the first time that you really get introduced to the concept that there are good and bad Predators. There's no monolithic idea of how they all operate within the universe, just like there's no monolithic idea of how all humanity operates within the universe. So being able to decipher who's good and who's bad is difficult. You can't judge a book by its cover anymore. You have to take a step back and assess the situation with a bit more nuance and a bit more intelligence before you just start pulling out guns and firing at anything that looks like it's bad.

**Why is Rory so important to Traeger?**
First of all, I love Jacob Tremblay, who plays Rory, because he's so cute. It's just ridiculous!

Rory has information and he is able to understand the Predators' language. He has a mathematical mind that's able to comprehend things that have been beyond the comprehension of Stargazer: how to locate the Predator ship, how to open the Predator ship. This kid is the key to the Predator technology. He knows where the ship is. He also knows how to open it and he may even know what's inside of it. He has a way of just seeing things and figuring things out that have escaped us to this point in time. And that's mainly because of his autism.

▶

## "I FELT THAT TRAEGER IS OPERATING ON THE OUTSIDE OF THE CAMARADERIE THAT'S TRANSPIRED AMONGST OUR LOONIES."

▶ **What does Jacob bring to the part of Rory?**
What I love about him is that he is incredibly precocious and is a kid first before he's an actor. His childhood, his youth, his innocence is still fully intact, even though he spends all this time on sets with adults who say bad words and swear! He knows what he's supposed to say and not supposed to say. He's a good kid.

We had this one scene in particular where he had to curse Traeger out. He had to call him an "asshole" and Shane would make him rehearse it over and over and over again and you could tell he's thinking, *I'm not supposed to be saying this, but it's in the script.* At one point in time, we were sitting in the car before we get out and he's like, "I don't really think that you're an a-hole. I just want you to know that." And I said, "Jacob, it's okay. For this scene, you can think I'm the biggest a-hole in the world." He replied, "Okay, I will. But I don't really think that you are." I was like, "I got you. But you can think it right now." He's like, "I got you. But I don't."

Shane had a couple of takes where he wanted Jacob to call me a "fuck face" and you can see like the first time that he said it, he was thinking, *Is my mom here?* He was thinking that it was not cool, but the director was telling him to say it. He did it over and over again, and when it was over, you could feel like the energy in his body had been sapped out because he's been doing something so wrong. He's just cute, man.

**Did you enjoy working with such a tight-knit group?**
It was good. I felt that Traeger is operating on the outside of the camaraderie that's transpired amongst our loonies. That's okay because he's sort of a lone wolf in his trajectory throughout the film. The person I probably interacted with most was Casey, Olivia Munn's character. That's been a great experience. I barely saw any of the other soldiers throughout the course of the film, because Traeger's focus was different.

**You have some tough scenes with Olivia Munn. How did they play out on set?**
Olivia's wonderful. We had one scene in particular that was somewhat confrontational and it was written really well, but it didn't quite make sense to me. I asked Shane what he thought I should do to end this particular scene and he said, "You know, I think what you're doing is great." I said, "Okay, cool. I'm gonna try something that's completely and totally inappropriate and probably won't work." He said, "Those are my favorite choices." So I was doing a scene where I'm attempting to intimidate her and she doesn't want to give up the goods. So I did

something strange: I just crept up on her, and sat on her lap. I got really close and let her know firmly that she will comply. Shane came over and said, "Okay. That works!" Olivia was totally cool with how it went. You always want to make sure you are respectful to your fellow actors.

**What do you think of Shane's writing and the way he makes characters feel so real?**
I think he recognizes that the script is a blueprint and we know that we need to hit specific marks in order to inform the audiences about certain things and to drive the plot. He encourages, and almost demands, that the actors break from the script and do what they feel is authentic and in the moment. There's a combination of these two things: this wonderful railroad track that he's already laid out for us, and then the encouragement to play within the frame of those railroad tracks.

What you hear in the film is more than likely going to be about 50 percent dialogue and then 50 percent what's coming off the actor's head in that moment.

*The Predator* **is funny and scary. What genre is this movie?**
All of life is everything, so I think the laughs pull the audience in. They get engaged in warning and rooting

**01** Sterling K. Brown as Traeger. (See previous spread)

**02** Traeger in trouble.

**03** Traeger takes a seat in a moment improvised by Brown.

**04** Rory, McKenna and Traeger aboard the Predator ship.

for the characters within the course of the film so when the thrills and the horror come, you care about the people. You've laughed with the people, you've lived with the people. When the people are going through something that's traumatic, now it's not just thrills for the sake of thrills. You want these people to succeed.

**What were the sets like to work on?**
Stargazer is ridiculous. The production value on this joint is off the chain – from the Predator spaceship to Stargazer. I'm used to the world of television, and so to come and play on a set of this magnitude has been really amazing. It takes your breath away. Sometimes I just go onto the set and walk around just for the hell of it – because when will I get another chance to do something like that?

On the Stargazer set there is a directory that tells you where everything is inside of the complex. One little touchstone is there's a gift shop! I love that humor.

**You also filmed on the Predator ship. How did that compare?**
I felt like Jonah in the belly of a whale. It was built for someone who's larger than myself, but it was my first time in a spaceship of any kind. It was cool to be in there with Jacob, too. I saw the kid in him. He was like a pig in slop! He was just jumping around on everything, pulling on wires. We were all just enjoying it as actors. We were getting paid to play on a spaceship! That's cool!

**What was it like working with the actors in the Predator suits?**
They're giant human beings that put on suits that make them even larger. It was so crazy to see them breathe and see the way the suit moves with them. The design of the costumes is incredible. Up close, it doesn't look fake, it looks like alien skin. You can see the breathing going back and forth. Once the stunts begin, they're like these gigantic parkour athletes that are capable of amazing things. I didn't know people that big can move like that.

**Who are the protagonists in this film?**
At the beginning, you don't know if you're rooting for our Marines because they're not all good. And then, you don't know whether or not you're rooting for the Predator once you realize there are two opposing factions.

**Do you think this film will resonate with fans of the original?**
It's interesting because it's so different. I think for fans of the original, there is gonna be an air of nostalgia. There are Easter eggs planted throughout the film for people who have seen the previous installments, but the tone is completely different on this one. I think the Easter eggs sort of bring in the fans from the past, but the tone really speaks to today's audience. The hope is that you bring in new people while maintaining the folks who have been fans of the past. ⚠

# TREVANTE RHODES
# WILLIAMS

Already box-office royalty, having played the lead in Oscar-winning movie *Moonlight*,
Trevante Rhodes is coming face-to-face with his childhood nightmare in
*The Predator*.

What did you know about the *Predator* movies before you signed on to this film?
I knew that it was frightening to me. I first saw *Predator* when I was about six or seven years old, and I remember it being the reason why I stopped watching anything remotely scary. I literally haven't watched scary movies since I was about seven years old because of this movie!

What was it you found so terrifying?
Just the idea of this thing that's kind of human – but also alien! And it wants to kill us... The realism of that is frightening to me still. I had a ridiculous imagination as a child, so I had nightmares for days...

What did you love about your character?
I had just signed on to do this other film in which I played a soldier, and this was kind of an extension of that person who had PTSD. It was interesting to have the opportunity to further the experience of being a soldier and explore what happens afterwards. In my mind, Williams is someone who has had these traumatizing moments. I wanted to experience being such a self-deprecating individual, because I'm actually heavily confident!

This is the kind of role I always look for – where I can pull on that emotional cord and show a different facet of an individual who is seen as a hardened, stone cold killer. I like having the opportunity to show the art of that.

Do Williams' tattoos have any significance?
Each tattoo is memorabilia – they are a journey of his life. He has tattoos on each of his fingers that say sorry. In my mind it's because he's saying sorry to the unit that he got killed for making a bad call. There's a question mark on the inside of his wrist because he ends up attempting to commit suicide – it's his contemplation of that.

Then he has a barbed wire strand around his arm with the names of his unit members. He has the American flag because he's still patriotic. On the inside he has DNR, which means Do Not Resuscitate. He also has an assault rifle on his forearm – that was the first tattoo he got, just because he was 18 years old and it was cool!

Tell us about this group of guys.
They're a collective of different yet so very alike individuals in the sense that we are all longing for that connection, longing for that brotherhood that we all had at one point in time – but we were taken out of it for whatever reason. In Nebraska's case, his unit was killed. Others may have just killed other people in unsavory ways. Others may have just been discharged because of mental ailments or whatever.

But we are all just this collective that met each other in this rehab center for vets suffering from PTSD. It's just a completely unique, different group of personalities. It's interesting to see how we are all so distinct. And we're all from different branches of the military as well, which also helps create an interesting conversation, because they don't always get along.

In doing research in preparing for the role I had the opportunity to speak to a bunch of wonderful people. Every person would tell me of instances of contemplating suicide. The memories and the flashbacks and the terrible emotions you feel from knowing that you've done these things and knowing that you've been ▶

## "I LIKE MOVIES THAT ARE IMMERSIVE. I REALLY APPRECIATE SOMEONE LEAVING THINGS TO THE IMAGINATION."

▶ a part of these things that you don't always agree with. But it's your orders; it's what your superiors tell you to do. It's really interesting.

**Why is the Assassin Predator so terrifying?**
The bigger things are, the more frightening they are. But the upgrade is so frightening because it is closer to a human. The further we get along in evolution, the scarier things get because eventually it gets to the point where something's indestructible.

This is the furthest along we've ever seen anything, because the original Predators are way more advanced than us, and they're afraid of this thing!

**What was it like meeting an actor in full Predator gear?**
It's insanity, man! Brian and Kyle play the emissaries of all the Predators. They are seven-foot guys and, in a sense, they're aliens because that in itself is unique. But then they put on these costumes with the long nails and they're so good at embodying the mannerisms and the walk and everything, it's just really freaky.

**What was it like working with Boyd Holdbrook and figuring out how that was going to work?**
I don't really have any other way to work other than to just be honest with people, and to be honest in front of the camera. You incorporate the same relationship that you have on the screen in real life, so it's not like having to try and turn something on. It's genuine, and the audience can sense that.

So with Boyd, we got dinner together, spent time together. We all value each other's processes, so it was really just about being open and honest. It's a collaborative thing on all sides of the coin. We all chime in together, and so it was just about understanding that.

**Why were you so excited about working with Shane Black?**
When you think about classic Hollywood, Shane Black is someone who, in a sense, created this action buddy genre. At a young age, he wrote *Lethal Weapon*.

That man is brilliant and he's been brilliant for a long time. It's so hard to sustain for five years in this industry, let alone 30!

**What did you respond to in *The Predator* script?**
I like movies that are immersive. I really appreciate someone leaving things to the imagination, and in the script that's how it was. I knew that Shane was going to cast a collective of actors who would fill in those blanks beautifully. Knowing that the script was by Shane Black, and knowing that he is a genius, I knew that this film would be aesthetically really cool.

And the story at the base of it, you're rooting for this absurd situation by making it about this dad trying to save his son. That's beautiful to me; What dad wouldn't do that in a perfect world? But then he meets this group of ridiculous people who are, at the same time, wounded and hurt and longing for certain things themselves. There are just so many pieces that he's just masterfully corralling so beautifully.

**Is this movie going to terrify people?**
Absolutely, this movie's gonna scare the mess out of people. It's bigger and better and badder! If the original film was scary to you, this is gonna be 10 times scarier. But hopefully it will also make people laugh. ⚠

03

02

**01** Trevante Rhodes as Williams. (See previous spread)

**02** A moment of levity. Rhodes feels that genuine relationships are key to making the characters work.

**03** Rhodes was pleased to work with Shane Black.

**04** Heavy artillery – Williams' unbridled assault.

# JAKE BUSEY
# DR. SEAN KEYES

Jake Busey's connection to the Predator is one of blood — his own father, Gary, played Peter Keyes in *Predator 2*. In *The Predator*, he plays the son of Keyes, who is continuing his father's work.

**What appealed to you the most about this project?**
I've known Shane [Black] for quite some time and always wanted to be in one of his films. The fact that it's *The Predator* and it's a sequel to a film that my dad was in; it's so many great things all wrapped into one package. I was really excited to be a part of it.

**Who do you play and how does he fit into the story?**
The character I play in this is Dr. Sean Keyes, and he's a research scientist who's devoted his life to finding out more about these Predators that are coming to our planet. He's trying to learn their whereabouts, their motives, their intent, and what they're up to on a deeper level than we've seen. He's trying to go deeper than what we know about them on the surface.

**What's Project Stargazer?**
Project Stargazer is one of these government facilities. It's an underground group who is secretly studying the alien traffic back and forth and studying the Predator aliens. I don't know if Stargazer would be considered good guys or not...

**Can you touch on the scale of Stargazer and what you were most impressed by?**
I'd say the thing that I've been most impressed by as far as the Stargazer set-up is our facility. There's a water treatment plant that's actually a Predator studification plant. The facility itself is quite impressive. It's grand. It's huge.

You look at all these films that are being made where they're strictly using a green screen, so the actors are having to pretend that they're on sets like this. With this, we're really there – we're in those three dimensions, and it's great because we have a visceral connection to the environment. We were happy about that.

**What makes the Predator creature iconic?**
I think one of the things that makes the Predator creature iconic is he stands for the unknown adversary – the adversary that you can't beat. It's symbolic – it's the fight that can't be won. As humans, we are constantly fighting larger and larger hurdles, and the Predator is always there, never to be defeated. Never to be outsmarted.

You combine that with the filmmakers who made the original movies and the actors who were in the original films and it was quite impressive. But the Predator itself has remained an unbeatable adversary. It comes from an unknown place that we're still unaware of. This, of course, is what my character, Dr. Sean Keyes, is trying to figure out.

**How would you describe the Predator to someone who has never seen it?**
I would describe the Predator as being breathtaking. You look at it and you're awestruck. The Predator-ness of it is very intimidating. Extremely intimidating. It's over seven feet tall and has those giant dreadlocks. It's so imposing. ▶

## "[SEAN KEYES] IS SEARCHING FOR ANSWERS. WHAT HAPPENED TO HIS FATHER AND WHY?"

**01** Jack Busey as the scientist seeking answers – Dr. Sean Keyes. (See previous spread)

**02** Bracket and Keyes come face to face with the species that killed his father.

**03** Sometimes the cost of seeking the truth can be high...

▶ As an actor, what is it like to take on the role of the son of a character which your own father played?

There have been a lot of roles that I've been fortunate to play – but to play the son of a character that my father played is pretty close to home. It's like playing myself in a fictional world. As fathers and sons go, you'll notice that most sons don't emulate or mimic their fathers. They tend to sort of bounce in the other direction. So my father's character, Peter Keyes, was a very intense, very driven, very manic character. Sean Keyes is more of a devoted scientist who's after the facts. He's really searching for some answers, searching for what happened to his father and why. Why was his father killed? And there's retribution that's being sought in that. ⚠

# WORLD BUILDING
## DESIGNING *THE PREDATOR*

From alien ships to advanced laboratories to small-town street scenes, the environments of *The Predator* merge the fantastical with the mundane. Production designer Martin Whist, set decorator Hamish Purdy, and supervising art director Michael Diner take us into their world.

**01** The fugitive Predator ship. (See previous spread)

**02** The fugitive Predator ship in landing site.

**03** Concept art for the interior of the Fugitive ship.

**04** The advanced alien ship breaking through Earth's atmosphere.

# THE FUGITIVE SHIP

**Martin Whist (production designer):** We shot on the stages at Mammoth Studios in Vancouver. We filled the stages to capacity, and over again! We had about 250,000 square feet. The exterior of the ark and the swamp upper set and the original pod crash are all on the same stage.

Something that I always have to deal with is multiple uses of sets. The ship set actually serves as two ships in the movie. It's the ship that the first Predator steals and it doubles as the pursuit ship which is what the Assassin Predator comes to Earth for.

The difference is pretty minimal. I didn't feel like there had to be a completely different ship. It's all part of the same society.

**Hamish Purdy (set decorator):** The ship was a very difficult set for us because we really didn't know what the finish line was. We knew what some of the challenges were based on the production illustrations. There was so much carving, sanding and painting to do that we were tight for time to get it ready. I prepped a lot of the alien technology that we keyed off of our Predator costume outside of the set. And then when it was time to install the details, I brought my crew and added all our LEDs to light the whole thing up. I think it came together quite well.

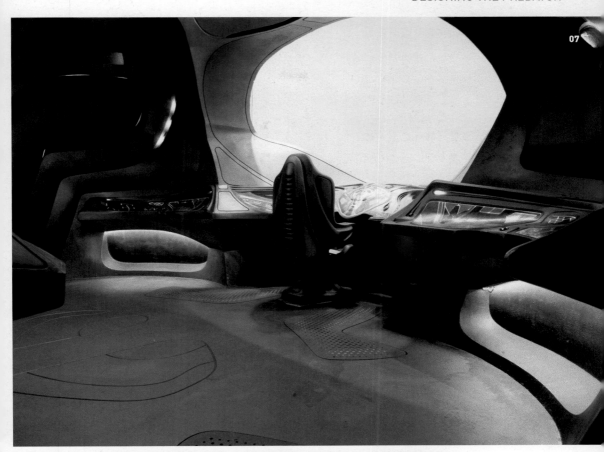

**05** Behind the scenes on the bridge of the fugitive Predator ship.

**06** A behind-the-scenes look at the lighting for the bridge.

**07** The pilot's seat for the alien vessel, with view screen. The final effects will be added in post-production.

**08** A behind-the-scenes shot of the finished set, carved, sanded and painted by Hamish Purdy and his team.

**09** The military guard
the Predator ship.

**10** Halloween in Rory's Neighborhood, but something's out of place...

**11** Concept art for Rory's basement, complete with old christmas decorations, multiple screens, and one mysterious alien mask.

# RORY'S NEIGHBORHOOD

**Martin Whist (production designer):** In my world, it goes from macro to micro. Everything's equally important, whether it's a big fancy lab, the inside of an RV, or Rory's basement. Everything is important.

**Hamish Purdy (set decorator):** A couple of specific sets got me really excited. Rory's basement, his inner sanctum, was a really exciting set to put together. We had a lot of time to prep it, so we were able to put a lot of layers in there.

Some sets you don't want to crowd with too many people getting involved. For example, with Rory's basement, I only wanted two people involved. If I got more people in there, there would be too many personalities in the set decoration.

DESIGNING *THE PREDATOR*

**12** Another side of Rory's basement. An old army uniform hangs at the back below the stairs.

**13** A behind the scenes look at building Rory's neighborhood.

**14** Trick or treaters take to the streets.

**15** An explosion in one of the houses brings disruption to the peaceful town.

**16** The helicopter approach to the Stargazer base.

**17** The helipad landing site for Stargazer base, above the river that runs through the base.

**18** Concept art of the outside approach to Stargazer lab.

**18** The inside of the surveillance room, with monitors spread around the walls.

# STARGAZER

**Michael Diner (supervising art director):** The Stargazer lab was a very large build. It's really two different environments: a high-tech American black ops world and the alien world. It was a completely lit, pre-built set. There were LED lights from top to bottom.

Our set director, Hamish Purdy, understood very quickly what was needed for Stargazer. He had complex elements that he was designing, and he was building these sort of high-tech beds and all of the lighting.

**Hamish Purdy (set decorator):** Stargazer is a round room. It's got five entrances and it is open to the stage ceiling. Round sets can very quickly become disorienting even if you know them intimately. You forget where the exit is unless you look closely. We were able to cheat with equipment quite a bit and hide things. You can get away with it in a set like that.

**Martin Whist (production designer):** Stargazer has the private contract to analyze these Predators. There is a curved hallway that goes through the doors, and an elevator. We're implying that there's much more to this facility under the dam than what we're actually seeing here.

The lab is the space in which the intense analysis takes place. There is a central bed which houses the Predator. It's a multiple-use functioning space for analysis built by Stargazer.

Stargazer is different to the military; they are not really working together. They are in alignment but Stargazer goes rogue, and turns out to be a greedy private corporation who wants to take control.

**20** A broad view of the circular lab, with various high-tech instruments scattered throughout.

# 01

PREDATOR LENS

58.47.22

ROLL: 100

SCENE: 429

TAKE: 1

DIRECTOR: SHANE BLACK
CAMERA: LARRY FONG ASC

# PRODUCING THE PREDATOR
## AN INTERVIEW WITH JOHN DAVIS

John Davis has been producing movies featuring the Predator for 30 years, starting with the 1987 classic. Now he's returning to oversee the most explosive entry into the franchise to date!

**W**here did your incredible journey producing the *Predator* movies start?

The original *Predator* was the first movie I ever produced. The Thomas Brothers had written it and somehow slipped it under my door. I was transitioning at the time from being an executive at Fox to being an independant producer. It was a great script, so we bought it. I had been the executive on *Commando*, and I was friends with Arnold Schwarzenegger. He invited me to come to the jungle with him to produce the movie, and at first, I was not sure... But then I thought about it: *A trip into the jungle with Arnold, hanging out with a bunch of bodybuilders, we're going to live in a luxury hotel and drive into the jungle every day... I'll do it!*

What was it about the original script that just resonated so strongly with you?

It was the idea of this creature from another planet that hunted the greatest game against the American commandos in the jungle. Even though the Predator had great brawn and weaponry and technology, there was an ingenuity and the desire to survive in man that made it a fair fight.

How was the iconic Predator created?

The original Predator was intitially played by Jean-Claude Van Damme. He was hired originally because the idea was that the Predator moved in the most graceful but aggressive way. Jean-Claude put the suit on

## "OVER THE COURSE OF A WEEKEND, STAN WINSTON DESIGNED WHAT BECAME THE PREDATOR."

and we were shooting for a day or so, and he started complaining about how hot the suit was and he really didn't want to do it anymore. So, we decided to get somebody else but somebody bigger in stature. We went to the creature designer, Stan Winston, and over the course of a weekend, Stan designed what became the Predator.

What made the new design work so well?

The greatest thing was the dreads because they really defined the creature. It was a humanoid to some extent and an alien to another extent. It was shocking, it was scary, it was interesting. There wasn't anything about it that was corny, and I think that's the hardest thing to do when you create an alien.

There had to be layers of reveal. It would be scariest if you didn't see the Predator for a long time. You felt his presence, you saw that Predator vision, and he was able to cloak himself. You saw what he was capable of doing as he slayed people, and then you got a glimpse. And then you got to see the helmet, and then finally you got to see what was underneath that helmet.

▶

**01** The Predator preparing for his close-up... (See previous spread)

**02** The humans pose for a photo with their alien co-star!

03

## "I THINK ALL ENTERTAINMENT IS DEFINED BY WHETHER IT IS FRESH OR NOT. SHANE IS ABLE TO COME UP WITH NEW IDEAS; THAT'S WHERE HIS BRAIN GOES."

▶ Why did that cast resonate so well at the time?
There are two governors that came out of that movie: Arnold and Jessie "The Body" Ventura. Shane Black was great in it. He was the first one killed by the Predator! Shane was brought in to do some work on the script. He didn't really want to do work on the script, so it was subterfuge. We thought we would bring him in, give him a part, and once we got him in Mexico we would get him to do a little bit of work. He had written *Lethal Weapon*, and he's an amazing writer. He was more interested in being an actor on this movie than a writer, so we decided he'd be the first killed!

And now he's back as writer and director...
It's ironic that he's come back to write and direct this because he has had a tremendous and long history with this franchise. Shane is a brilliant director. He's got a wicked sense of humor and an amazing way of observing things. I think that's why this script was so good and that's why this movie is so great.

What makes him such a good filmmaker?
He's a great student of movies. He's an encyclopedia. He has probably watched every great piece of storytelling in cinema history. In addition to that, he is an amazing storyteller. He has a wry sense of humor. He's got the ability to say if something has been done before, and figure out how to do it differently. I think all entertainment is defined by whether it is fresh or not. Shane is able to come up with new ideas; that's where his brain goes – that's when you get a great, exciting movie. Not only is the action great in this movie, it's inspired. Shane storyboarded this action and he did the animatics for a year to get it right. He worked laboriously with a whole staff of people scripting each little piece of action and how it would fit together. Then he filmed it, put music to it, and tore it apart and redid it again to get it right.

What was it like to watch the cast at work?
I would sit on the set and never quite know what I was going to see. There are six great actors playing the "loonies." It's the Dirty Dozen with loonies. I had no idea what they were going to say because Shane had changed the dialogue a few minutes before. They obviously fed off of each other because one had a new line and improvise a little, and then there were different reactions. I haven't seen that often, and I've shot many movies. It was great. A lot of actors are not comfortable with improvising. Many directors are not comfortable with a script that hasn't been set in stone four ▶

weeks before. To be able to spontaneously create material on a set both as a director and on behalf of the actors is something that Shane does so well.

**What makes the loonies such unlikely protagonists?**
This group of misfits from the Veterans Hosptial save the world. You really love each of them in their damaged state because nobody did it to themselves. The process of being at war did it to them and they are just trying to survive – but they are still pretty courageous, and they are looking for a great last act. There's something about people who have that extraordinary courage against those limitations. Maybe they're too crazy to be afraid when they should be, but they all have a certain amount of authenticity and heart. This is a great last quest for them. They're about to all be stored in a looney bin in a VA facility.

**How did you feel about the concept of having the Predators helping the humans?**
It made a lot of sense because the thing we all love about the Predator is that there was a code of honor. A hunter hunts but there are rules and there's a way it's done. As the Predator upgrades and society is changing its goals, there are basically purists who are not happy about this metamorphosis – that it's changing the order of things. There may well be a civil war going on within the ranks of the Predator world and community.

**Is humanity aware of the Predators?**
Certain people have definitely been aware since Dutch Schaefer survived his encounter with the Predator at the end of the first movie. Maybe it's top secret information, held by the government. We all know that a government easily corrupts itself and that evil people are somehow drawn to government. There is that evil

> **"CERTAIN PEOPLE HAVE DEFINITELY BEEN AWARE [OF THE PREDATOR] SINCE DUTCH SCHAEFER SURVIVED HIS ENCOUNTER AT THE END OF THE FIRST MOVIE."**

**03** Shane Black oversees a sequence with the captured Predator. (See previous spread)

**04** The Predators are skilled at all forms of combat.

**05** A Predator, loose in Stargazer labs...

subculture within a government. There is that group of people that believe they know better. There's a people who are driven by power, who are driven by money, who are driven by their own justification to be, and they are not part of the greater good as much as they are part of their own good.

We see this among government agencies and intelligence agencies all the time. This is another part of our government that can be corrupted. They have tremendous power. They have the knowledge, the weaponry, and the methods of how to fight these Predators because they've been captured over time and they've been studied.

**Why is *Predator* still such a popular franchise?**
I think this is one of those franchises that people love, and they've loved through the years. The very first *Predator* is still watched a lot. Its DVD sales are still high, and DVDs aren't even around anymore. It sells around the world on cable and over the streaming services. It's got such a big worldwide audience. It's hard to believe that 30 years later, this movie has continued to capture generation after generation. It's like my kids still listen to the Beatles. Young people love the Predator.

This is the franchise that you loved 30 years later. These are the consequences of what has happened. This is what has been going on in the last 30 years. It's a great story and I think it's a fun story. ⚠

# 05

# OTHER GREAT TIE-IN COMPANIONS FROM TITAN
## ON SALE NOW!

**Star Trek: The Movies**
ISBN 9781785855924

**Fifty Years of Star Trek**
ISBN 9781785855931

**Star Trek – A Next Generation Companion**
ISBN 9781785855948

**Star Trek Discovery Collector's Edition**
ISBN 9781785861581

**Star Wars: Lords of the Sith**
ISBN 9781785851919

**Star Wars: Heroes of the Force**
ISBN 9781785851926

**The Best of Star Wars Insider Volume 1**
ISBN 9781785851162

**The Best of Star Wars Insider Volume 2**
ISBN 9781785851179

**The Best of Star Wars Insider Volume 3**
ISBN 9781785851896

**...tar Wars ...me 4**
...1902

**Star Wars: Icons Of The Galaxy**
ISBN 9781785851933

**Star Wars: The Last Jedi The Official Collector's Edition**
ISBN 9781785862113

**Star Wars: The Last Jedi The Official Movie Companion**
ISBN 9781785863004

**Solo: A Star Wars Story The Official Movie Companion**
ISBN 9781785863011

**Black Panther Movie Special**
ISBN 9781785866531

**Ant-Man and the Wasp Movie Special**
ISBN 9781785868092

**Avengers: Infinity War Movie Special**
ISBN 9781785868054

## TITANCOMICS
### ...ore information visit www.titan-comics.com